PIGEON RACING

UNVEILED

Racing pigeons breeds, loft, feeding, health, training, racing, record keeping and systems

Freddie J.Craig

Freddie J.Craig

Table of Contents

This guide is dedicated to the tireless fanciers, whose passion and commitment

transform lofts into sanctuaries of dreams. May the wings of your pigeons carry

not just the weight of victories but also the spirit of camaraderie that defines the

extraordinary journey of pigeon racing.

"In the symphony of wings, every loft echoes with the harmony of dedication, every flight becomes a note of triumph, and every fancier, a conductor of dreams in the boundless skies of pigeon racing."

– Freddie J.Craig

Chapter 1: Introduction to Homing Pigeon Racing

A Deep Dive into the Allure

Homing pigeon racing, a sport that transcends the ordinary, captures the hearts of enthusiasts worldwide. In this chapter, we embark on a journey to unravel the fascination behind this unique pastime, exploring its history, the joy it brings to participants, and the magic that lies within the wings of these remarkable birds.

A Pictorial Glimpse into the Past

To understand the allure of homing pigeon racing, one must first delve into its rich history. Dating back to ancient times, pigeons were revered for their ability to carry messages across vast distances. From military communication to personal letters, these birds played a crucial role in connecting people separated by miles.

Fast forward to the 19th century, and homing pigeon racing emerged as a competitive sport. The concept was simple yet captivating: release pigeons from different locations and watch as they raced back to their lofts. The thrill of waiting for the first bird to return, carrying messages or simply proving its speed, ignited a passion that continues to burn brightly today.

The Numbers Game: Racing at its Core

At its core, homing pigeon racing is a numbers game—one that combines the precision of time with the unpredictability of nature. Consider this: in a major race, thousands of pigeons can be released simultaneously, each with the goal of reaching its loft before the others.

The excitement lies not only in the speed of the birds but also in the strategy employed by their handlers.

Let's break down the numbers. On average, racing pigeons can cover distances ranging from 100 to 600 miles in a single race. The record for the longest pigeon race, an astonishing 7,200 miles, emphasizes the incredible feats these birds can achieve. It's not just about distance; it's about endurance, navigation, and the unbreakable bond between the pigeon and its loft.

Passion Personified: The Pigeon Fancier's Perspective

To truly grasp the fascination of homing pigeon racing, one must step into the shoes of a pigeon fancier. These individuals, often referred to as "pigeon racers" or "fliers," invest not only time and money but also a piece of their hearts into their feathered companions.

Consider John, a seasoned pigeon racer who has been in the game for over a decade. For him, the thrill of watching his pigeons return home after a race is unparalleled. "It's not just a hobby; it's a lifestyle. The bond you share with your pigeons is indescribable," he says with a twinkle in his eye.

The passion goes beyond the thrill of competition. Pigeon fanciers develop deep connections with their birds, recognizing each one by its unique characteristics. It's a personal journey, where success is measured not only by victories on the racecourse but also by the health and happiness of the pigeons in their care.

The Science of Navigation: A Pigeon's Extraordinary Instincts

What sets homing pigeons apart is their uncanny ability to navigate across vast distances with unerring precision. Scientists have long been fascinated by this phenomenon, studying the pigeons' use of Earth's magnetic field, landmarks, and even the sun to find their way home.

Consider the classic "homing instinct" experiment conducted in the mid-20th century. Pigeons were transported in light-proof containers to locations hundreds of miles away. Astonishingly, when released, these birds found their way back home with astounding accuracy. This innate sense of direction, a combination of genetics and environmental cues, adds an extra layer of wonder to the world of homing pigeon racing.

A Global Community: The Thrill of International Competitions

Homing pigeon racing isn't confined to local communities; it's a global phenomenon that brings together individuals from diverse cultures and backgrounds. International competitions, where pigeons traverse borders and cross continents, showcase the universality of this passion.

In the annual South African Million Dollar Pigeon Race, for instance, participants from around the world send their pigeons to compete for a substantial cash prize. The race, spanning 500 kilometers, tests the mettle of both the pigeons and their handlers. It's not just a test of speed but also a celebration of unity, as individuals from different corners of the globe come together for the love of the sport.

Conclusion: The Timeless Allure of Homing Pigeon Racing

In conclusion, the fascination of homing pigeon racing lies in its rich history, the thrill of competition, the passion of its participants, the extraordinary instincts of the pigeons, and the global community it has fostered. Whether you're a seasoned pigeon fancier or a curious observer, the magic of watching these winged athletes take flight and return home is an experience that transcends time and borders.

Unveiling the Tapestry of Homing Pigeon Racing through History

In the vast realm of human-animal partnerships, few tales weave a narrative as rich and enduring as that of homing pigeon racing. As we step back in time, we uncover the fascinating history and evolution of this unique sport, tracing its roots from ancient civilizations to the modern, high-stakes competitions that capture the imagination of enthusiasts worldwide.

Ancient Messengers: Pigeons in Antiquity

Our journey through the annals of history begins in ancient Mesopotamia, where pigeons were employed as messengers over 3,000 years ago. The Persian Empire, recognizing the remarkable homing abilities of these birds, established a vast communication network using pigeon messengers.

Fast forward to ancient Greece, and we find historical records of pigeon racing during the Olympic Games. Pigeons carried news of victors and game results to distant cities, creating a spectacle that combined athleticism with avian grace.

The Pigeon Post of Genghis Khan: A Military Legacy

Pigeons played a pivotal role in military communications, particularly during the time of Genghis Khan and the Mongol Empire. The great Khan and his generals utilized pigeons as a reliable means of transmitting messages across vast territories, enabling swift coordination of troops and strategies.

To put the historical significance into perspective, consider this: Genghis Khan's pigeon post system is said to have covered a distance of over 6,000 miles, connecting the Mongol capital to the far reaches of the empire. This early application of pigeon racing principles laid the foundation for the sport's evolution over the centuries.

Pigeon Racing Takes Flight: 19th Century Beginnings

The 19th century witnessed the formalization of pigeon racing as a sport in Europe. The first recorded pigeon race took place in Belgium in 1818, marking the beginning of an era that would see the sport soar to new heights.

Belgium, often considered the birthplace of modern pigeon racing, established the first official pigeon racing club in 1850. The concept was simple yet revolutionary: release pigeons from different locations and race them back to their lofts. The thrill of competition, combined with the camaraderie among enthusiasts, fueled the rapid spread of pigeon racing across European countries.

Pigeon Racing Spreads its Wings: Global Expansion in the 20th Century

As the 20th century dawned, pigeon racing expanded its reach beyond European borders, finding fertile ground in North America, Australia, and beyond. Pigeon racing clubs proliferated, creating a global community of enthusiasts bound by a shared passion for these remarkable birds.

The year 1909 marked a historic moment in pigeon racing history with the establishment of the American Racing Pigeon Union (ARPU). This organization played a pivotal role in standardizing rules, promoting fair competition, and fostering a sense of unity among American pigeon fanciers.

War Heroes: Pigeons in World War I and II

The role of homing pigeons in military communications was reaffirmed during the World Wars. Pigeons, equipped with small canisters containing critical messages, were deployed by various armed forces to relay information across enemy lines.

One notable hero was Cher Ami, a carrier pigeon of the U.S. Army Signal Corps during World War I. Despite being injured in the line of duty, Cher Ami successfully delivered a crucial message, saving the lives of nearly 200 soldiers. This wartime contribution elevated the status of pigeons, emphasizing their intelligence and reliability.

Technological Advances: From Radios to GPS

The mid-20th century witnessed a fascinating intersection of tradition and technology within the world of pigeon racing. While the sport maintained its core principles, advancements such as electronic timing systems and radio communication added a new dimension to competitions.

Electronic timing systems, introduced in the 1970s, revolutionized the accuracy of race results. Each pigeon is equipped with a unique electronic band that records the exact time of its arrival, eliminating the margin of human error and adding a layer of precision to the sport.

Prestigious Competitions and Record-Breaking Feats

The world of pigeon racing is punctuated by prestigious competitions that showcase the speed, endurance, and navigation skills of these avian athletes. One such event is the Barcelona International One Loft Race, covering a staggering distance of over 700 miles. Pigeons from around the world compete in this ultimate test of stamina and strategy.

Records within the sport continue to be shattered. In 1995, a pigeon named "Blue Heaven" set a world record by covering a distance of 1,479 kilometers (919 miles) in a single race. Such feats not only highlight the remarkable capabilities of racing pigeons but also fuel the competitive spirit within the global pigeon racing community.

The Future of Pigeon Racing: Challenges and Innovations

As we approach the present day, pigeon racing faces both challenges and opportunities. Urbanization and changing landscapes pose threats to traditional racing routes, necessitating adaptations and innovations to ensure the continuity of the sport.

One notable development is the use of GPS technology in tracking and monitoring pigeon races. GPS-equipped backpacks allow enthusiasts to follow the journey of their pigeons in real-time, adding an interactive and tech-savvy element to the age-old tradition of racing.

Conclusion: A Tapestry Unfinished

In conclusion, the history and evolution of pigeon racing form a tapestry woven with threads of tradition, innovation, and a deep connection between humans and birds. From ancient civilizations to modern competitions, the sport has endured, adapting to the changing times while preserving its essence.

Exploring the Enriching Benefits of Racing Pigeons as a Hobby

In a world brimming with hobbies and pastimes, racing pigeons stand out as more than just feathered competitors; they become companions in a journey filled with excitement, camaraderie, and a deep connection to nature. In this exploration of the benefits of racing pigeons as a hobby, we uncover the physical, mental, and emotional rewards that make this avian pursuit a source of joy for enthusiasts around the globe.

Physical Fitness and Outdoor Engagement

Engaging in pigeon racing necessitates a level of physical activity that extends beyond the usual bounds of hobbyist pursuits. Pigeon fanciers find themselves involved in activities such as building and maintaining pigeon lofts, handling and caring for the birds, and participating in training exercises. These activities contribute to increased physical fitness, providing a welcome contrast to sedentary lifestyles.

Consider the routine of a pigeon racer: from overseeing the loft's construction to releasing pigeons for training flights, each task involves movement and outdoor engagement. According to a study conducted by the American Heart Association, activities like these contribute to improved cardiovascular health, reduced stress levels, and enhanced overall well-being.

Bonding with Nature: A Therapeutic Escape

In a world dominated by screens and concrete, the hobby of racing pigeons offers a therapeutic escape into nature. Pigeon fanciers often find solace in the rhythmic cooing of their birds, the feel of the wind on their faces during training sessions, and the simple joy of observing these creatures in flight.

A study published in the Journal of Environmental Psychology emphasizes the positive impact of nature-based activities on mental health. The calming effects of being in natural surroundings, combined with the companionship of racing pigeons, create a symbiotic relationship that promotes emotional well-being and a sense of connection to the natural world.

Community and Camaraderie: Fostering Social Bonds

Pigeon racing is not merely an individual pursuit; it thrives on the sense of community and camaraderie that emerges among enthusiasts. Pigeon clubs and associations bring together individuals with a shared passion for these winged athletes, fostering a supportive network where experiences, tips, and stories are exchanged.

Participating in pigeon racing competitions becomes more than a quest for victory; it transforms into a communal event where friendships are forged and a sense of belonging prevails. According to a survey conducted by the National Institute of Mental Health, social connections are integral to mental health, providing emotional support and a sense of purpose.

Mental Stimulation and Strategic Thinking

Training and racing pigeons require more than physical effort; they demand strategic thinking, problem-solving, and meticulous planning. Pigeon fanciers engage in activities such as designing race routes, determining feeding regimens, and analyzing flight patterns—a mental workout that stimulates cognitive functions.

A study published in the Journal of Aging and Health highlights the cognitive benefits of engaging in mentally challenging hobbies. The constant evaluation of race strategies, the monitoring of pigeon health, and the anticipation of flight patterns contribute to mental agility, providing enthusiasts with a fulfilling and intellectually stimulating pastime.

Educational Opportunities for All Ages

Racing pigeons as a hobby offer unique educational opportunities for individuals of all ages. Children, in particular, can benefit from learning about avian biology, navigation, and responsible pet ownership through their involvement in caring for and training pigeons.

Pigeon racing also provides a platform for exploring scientific concepts such as genetics, instinct, and adaptation. For example, breeding programs aimed at enhancing specific traits in racing pigeons offer practical lessons in genetics and selective breeding.

Financial Incentives and Economic Impact

While the primary motivation for engaging in pigeon racing is often the love of the sport, there are financial incentives that add an extra layer of appeal. Prestigious competitions often come with substantial cash prizes, creating an opportunity for pigeon fanciers to not only indulge in their passion but also potentially earn income through successful racing.

Furthermore, the economic impact of pigeon racing extends beyond individual enthusiasts. Pigeon feed and equipment suppliers, loft construction services, and event organizers all contribute to a thriving industry. According to a report by the International Federation of Pigeon Racing, the economic ripple effect of the sport encompasses various sectors, supporting local businesses and communities.

Intergenerational Bonding and Family Values

Pigeon racing has a unique ability to transcend generations, creating opportunities for intergenerational bonding. Families often come together to share in the responsibilities of caring for pigeons, training them, and participating in races. This shared experience fosters a sense of unity and reinforces family values.

Consider the story of the Smith family, where grandparents, parents, and grandchildren are actively involved in pigeon racing. The sport becomes a thread that weaves through family gatherings, providing a shared interest that spans age groups and promotes the passing down of knowledge and traditions.

Global Connectivity: A Shared Passion Across Borders

In an era defined by global connectivity, pigeon racing serves as a bridge that connects enthusiasts across borders and cultures. International competitions bring together participants from diverse backgrounds, fostering a sense of unity and mutual respect among individuals who share a common love for these remarkable birds.

The Global Pigeon Racing Community, an online platform connecting pigeon fanciers worldwide, exemplifies this global camaraderie. Enthusiasts from different continents share insights, stories, and advice, transcending geographical boundaries and creating a virtual community that celebrates the universal appeal of pigeon racing.

Conclusion: Soaring Beyond the Race Track

In conclusion, the benefits of racing pigeons as a hobby extend far beyond the race track. From physical fitness and mental stimulation to community building and global connectivity, pigeon racing offers a multifaceted experience that enriches the lives of enthusiasts. As we celebrate the joy of watching these winged athletes take flight, let us also acknowledge the profound impact they have on the well-being, relationships, and sense of purpose of those who embrace the hobby.

An In-Depth Overview of Pigeon Breeds Ideal for Racing

In the world of pigeon racing, the choice of the right breed can make all the difference between an average performance and a champion flyer. This chapter delves into the diverse array of pigeon breeds suitable for racing, exploring their unique characteristics, strengths, and historical significance in the exhilarating sport of homing pigeon racing.

1. Homing Pigeon (Columba livia)

Characteristics:

- Recognized for their intelligence and homing instincts.
- Sleek and aerodynamic body, ideal for long-distance flights.
- Varied colorations, including solid colors, pied patterns, and markings.

Performance:

- Exceptional navigators with the ability to cover long distances.
- Known for their speed and endurance, making them a popular choice for racing.

The homing pigeon, also known as the racing pigeon, is the quintessential breed for the sport. Bred specifically for its homing ability, these pigeons exhibit an innate sense of direction, enabling them to find their way back to their lofts from considerable distances. Their adaptability to various racing conditions, combined with their intelligence and speed, makes them the go-to choice for pigeon racers worldwide.

2. Sion Pigeon

Characteristics:

- Compact and muscular build.
- Short beak and a distinctive head shape.
- Variety of colors, including blues, reds, and yellows.

Performance:

- Renowned for their agility and quick reflexes.
- Suitable for shorter distance races due to their burst of speed.

The Sion pigeon, originating from Belgium, is prized for its agility and rapid acceleration. While not known for long-distance racing, Sion pigeons excel in shorter races where quick reflexes and burst speed are crucial. Their unique appearance, coupled with their competitive spirit, makes them a favorite among pigeon fanciers participating in sprint-style competitions.

3. Birmingham Roller

Characteristics:

- Compact and muscular body.
- Short beak and expressive eyes.
- Varieties in color, including black, red, and blue.

Performance:

- Specialized in acrobatic mid-air rolls.
- Suited for competitions focusing on performance and style.

The Birmingham Roller stands out for its unique talent in mid-air acrobatics. While not a long-distance racer, these pigeons excel in competitions that emphasize performance and style. During flights, they execute somersaults and rolls, showcasing a captivating display of aerobatic skill. Enthusiasts often participate in roller competitions, where the precision and complexity of the rolls determine the winner.

4. Janssen Pigeon

Characteristics:

- Medium-sized with a robust build.
- Red or blue plumage with white flight feathers.
- Known for their strong wings and endurance.

Performance:

- Renowned for long-distance racing.
- Exceptional endurance and the ability to cover extensive distances.

The Janssen pigeon, hailing from Belgium, is celebrated for its endurance and long-distance racing capabilities. With a robust build and powerful wings, Janssen pigeons are well-suited for competitions that demand stamina and the ability to cover extensive distances. Their remarkable performances in marathon-style races have made them a sought-after breed among serious pigeon racers.

5. Flor Engels Pigeon

Characteristics:

- Medium-sized with a compact and athletic build.
- Varied colorations, including blue, red, and yellow.
- Known for their keen intelligence and adaptability.

Performance:

- Versatile performers suitable for various race distances.
- Renowned for their adaptability to different weather conditions.

The Flor Engels pigeon, originating from the Netherlands, is prized for its versatility and adaptability. With a compact and athletic build, these pigeons perform well in races of varying distances. Their keen intelligence and ability to adapt to different weather conditions make them a reliable choice for pigeon fanciers seeking a versatile and competitive breed.

6. Modena Pigeon

Characteristics:

- Distinctive body shape with a short beak.
- Varieties in color, including black, blue, and red.
- Known for their elegant appearance and ornamental value.

Performance:

- Suited for shorter races.
- Preferred for their aesthetic appeal and unique appearance.

The Modena pigeon, recognized for its distinctive appearance, is often chosen for its ornamental value. While not a specialized racer for long distances, Modena pigeons are suitable for shorter races and are favored for their elegant and unique aesthetic. Enthusiasts who appreciate the blend of performance and beauty often find the Modena pigeon to be a delightful addition to their racing team.

7. Tippler Pigeon

Characteristics:

- Medium-sized with a slender and elongated body.
- Varieties in color, including black, red, and yellow.
- Known for their exceptional endurance and prolonged flight times.

Performance:

- Specialized in endurance flying.
- Suited for competitions focused on flight duration.

The Tippler pigeon, prized for its exceptional endurance, is specialized in prolonged flight times. While not renowned for top-speed racing, Tipplers excel in competitions that emphasize endurance and flight duration. Enthusiasts who appreciate the spectacle of pigeons soaring for extended periods find the Tippler breed to be a captivating addition to their racing team.

Conclusion: Tailoring the Team for Triumph

In conclusion, the world of pigeon racing offers a diverse palette of breeds, each with its unique characteristics and strengths. Whether aiming for speed, endurance, or a blend of performance and style, pigeon fanciers can tailor their racing teams to suit specific competitions and personal preferences.

From the iconic homing pigeon to the acrobatic Birmingham Roller and the enduring Janssen, each breed contributes to the dynamic and thrilling landscape of pigeon racing. As enthusiasts embark on their racing endeavors, the careful selection of breeds becomes a strategic element in the pursuit of victory and the enjoyment of this timeless and captivating hobby.

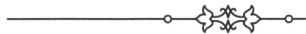

Chapter 2: Getting Started with Racing Pigeons

Crafting the Perfect Pigeon Loft - A Comprehensive Guide

Embarking on the journey of pigeon racing requires more than just a love for these feathered athletes; it demands a well-designed and meticulously planned pigeon loft. In this exploration of setting up a pigeon loft, we delve into the essential aspects of design, construction, and management to create a haven where racing pigeons can thrive and reach their full potential.

1. Loft Design: Creating a Pigeon Paradise

Space Considerations:

- The loft should provide ample space for pigeons to move, stretch their wings, and engage in natural behaviors.
- A minimum of 2 square feet of loft space per pigeon is recommended for optimal comfort.

Orientation and Ventilation:

- The loft should be positioned to receive ample sunlight and natural airflow.
- Adequate ventilation is crucial to prevent respiratory issues. Consider the installation of adjustable vents to regulate airflow.

Security Measures:

- Implement secure doors and windows to protect pigeons from predators.
- Ensure the loft is constructed with sturdy materials to withstand weather conditions and external threats.

Creating a comfortable and secure environment is the foundation of a successful pigeon loft. Pigeons thrive in lofts that mimic their natural habitats, allowing them to exhibit their innate behaviors and fostering overall well-being.

2. Loft Construction: Materials and Considerations

Materials:

- Choose durable and weather-resistant materials for construction, such as pressure-treated wood or metal.
- The loft's roof should be waterproof to protect pigeons from the elements.

Insulation:

- Consider insulating the loft to regulate temperature extremes, providing a comfortable environment for pigeons in all seasons.

Flooring:

- Use materials for the loft floor that are easy to clean and disinfect, such as sealed concrete or removable trays.

Constructing a pigeon loft involves careful consideration of materials to ensure longevity, weather resistance, and ease of maintenance. A well-insulated and strategically designed loft provides a stable and comfortable habitat for racing pigeons.

3. Loft Features: Providing for Pigeon Comfort

Nesting Boxes:

- Install nesting boxes with adequate space for pigeons to lay eggs and care for their young.
- Ensure easy access for cleaning and monitoring.

Perches and Roosts:

- Incorporate perches at varying heights to accommodate pigeons' natural instincts to roost.
- Use smooth, rounded perches to prevent foot injuries.

Feeding and Watering Stations:

- Designate specific areas for feeding and watering, ensuring easy access for pigeons.
- Install feeders and water containers that are easy to clean and sanitize regularly.

The layout of the loft plays a crucial role in catering to the natural behaviors of racing pigeons. Nesting boxes, perches, and feeding stations should be strategically placed to provide comfort, security, and easy maintenance.

4. Loft Management: Cleaning and Hygiene

Regular Cleaning Schedule:

- Establish a routine for cleaning the loft to maintain a hygienic environment.

- Remove droppings, old nesting materials, and debris regularly to prevent the spread of diseases.

Disinfection Practices:

- Use pigeon-friendly disinfectants to clean and sanitize the loft.
- Implement a quarantine process for new pigeons to prevent the introduction of diseases.

Health Monitoring:

- Monitor the health of pigeons regularly, paying attention to signs of illness.
- Isolate sick pigeons promptly to prevent the spread of diseases within the loft.

Maintaining a clean and hygienic loft is paramount for the health and well-being of racing pigeons. A disciplined cleaning schedule, proper disinfection practices, and vigilant health monitoring contribute to a thriving loft environment.

5. Loft Automation: Embracing Technology

Automatic Feeding Systems:

- Invest in automatic feeders to ensure a consistent and controlled diet for racing pigeons.
- These systems can be programmed to dispense feed at specific intervals, promoting a regular feeding schedule.

Temperature Control:

- Install climate control systems, such as heaters or fans, to regulate temperature extremes.
- Maintaining a stable and comfortable temperature is essential for pigeon well-being.

Remote Monitoring:

- Explore technological solutions for remote monitoring of the loft.
- Cameras and sensors can provide real-time insights into pigeon behavior, aiding in health assessment and loft management.

Embracing technology in loft management can streamline processes, enhance efficiency, and contribute to the overall well-being of racing pigeons. Automated systems and remote monitoring tools offer convenience while ensuring that pigeons receive optimal care.

6. Loft Aesthetics: Balancing Beauty and Functionality

Landscaping and Surroundings:

- Consider the aesthetic appeal of the loft surroundings.
- Landscaping with greenery and providing a visually pleasing environment contributes to the well-being of both pigeons and enthusiasts.

Customization:

- Personalize the loft with artistic touches that reflect the owner's passion for pigeon racing.
- Murals, signage, and decorative elements can transform the loft into a unique and inviting space.

Creating a visually appealing loft adds a personal touch to the racing pigeon hobby. Balancing functionality with aesthetics enhances the overall experience for both pigeons and enthusiasts.

Conclusion: Elevating the Pigeon Loft Experience

In conclusion, setting up a pigeon loft involves a delicate balance of design, construction, and management. A well-designed loft provides racing pigeons with a secure, comfortable, and stimulating environment, setting the stage for success on the racecourse.

Whether it's considering space, materials, or incorporating technological advancements, each element contributes to the overall well-being and performance of racing pigeons. As enthusiasts embark on the journey of pigeon racing, the loft becomes not just a functional space but a haven where the wings of these remarkable athletes can soar to new heights.

A Guide to Selecting Healthy and Fit Racing Pigeons

In the world of pigeon racing, success hinges not only on training and loft management but also on the selection of healthy and fit racing pigeons. This chapter delves into the intricacies of choosing pigeons that are not just feathered athletes but embody the pinnacle of health, vitality, and the innate qualities that make them champions on the racecourse.

1. Understanding the Basics: What Makes a Healthy Pigeon?

Physical Attributes:

- Vibrant and glossy plumage is a sign of overall health.
- Bright and alert eyes indicate good vitality.
- Well-groomed and clean feathers reflect proper self-maintenance.

Body Condition:

- The pigeon should have a well-muscled and firm body.
- The breast muscles, essential for sustained flight, should be strong and developed.

Weight and Size:

- Pigeons of moderate weight and size are generally healthier and more agile.
- Obesity or excessive leanness can indicate underlying health issues.

The first step in selecting racing pigeons is a keen understanding of the basic indicators of health. Examining the physical attributes, body condition, and weight of a pigeon provides valuable insights into its overall well-being.

2. Pigeon Pedigree: Examining Ancestral Lineage

Champion Bloodlines:

- Investigate the pedigree of potential racing pigeons.
- Pigeons with a lineage of successful racers often inherit favorable traits.

Family History:

- Assess the racing history of siblings and parents.
- Consistent performance within a family line is a positive indicator of genetic prowess.

Genetic Diversity:

- Balance the pursuit of champion bloodlines with the importance of genetic diversity.
- A diverse gene pool enhances the adaptability and resilience of racing pigeons.

Examining the pedigree of racing pigeons provides valuable insights into their genetic potential. Champion bloodlines and a history of successful racers within the family contribute to the likelihood of producing high-performing offspring.

3. Health Checks: A Pigeon Physical Examination

Feather Quality:

- Check for smooth, well-groomed feathers without signs of moulting or stress.
- Feather quality is a direct reflection of a pigeon's overall health and nutrition.

Breathing and Respiration:

- Observe the pigeon's breathing for any signs of wheezing or labored respiration.
- Healthy pigeons should exhibit steady and regular breathing patterns.

Eyes and Nostrils:

- Clear and bright eyes indicate good health.
- Nostrils should be clean, dry, and free from any discharge.

Conducting a thorough physical examination is crucial in assessing the immediate health of a racing pigeon. Observing feather quality, respiratory patterns, and the condition of eyes and nostrils provides crucial information for potential health issues.

4. Vital Statistics: Evaluating Performance Metrics

Wing Length:

- Measure the length of the primary flight feathers (wing length).
- Longer wings are associated with increased endurance and efficiency in flight.

Heart Rate:

- Monitor the pigeon's heart rate during periods of rest and activity.
- A well-conditioned racing pigeon will have a lower resting heart rate and the ability to quickly recover after exertion.

Metabolic Rate:

- Assess the pigeon's metabolic rate through observation of energy levels and feeding habits.
- Pigeons with efficient metabolisms are more likely to maintain stamina during races.

Evaluating vital statistics such as wing length, heart rate, and metabolic efficiency provides quantitative insights into a pigeon's potential for high-performance racing. These metrics contribute to the selection process by identifying individuals with physical attributes conducive to endurance and efficiency.

5. Behavioral Traits: The Spirit of a Champion

Alertness and Curiosity:

- Healthy racing pigeons exhibit a natural curiosity and alertness to their surroundings.
- A pigeon that is engaged and observant is likely to have a high level of mental and physical fitness.

Territorial Instincts:

- Observe the pigeon's territorial behavior, a sign of a strong and assertive nature.
- Pigeons with a well-defined sense of territory are more likely to navigate race routes confidently.

Social Interaction:

- Evaluate the pigeon's ability to interact with loft mates and handlers.
- Pigeons that engage positively in social interactions demonstrate a balanced and adaptable temperament.

Behavioral traits are integral to the overall health and fitness of racing pigeons. Observing alertness, territorial instincts, and social interactions provides insights into a pigeon's mental well-being and its ability to cope with the demands of racing.

6. Age Considerations: Striking the Right Balance

Young Birds:

- Young pigeons (yearlings) may have untapped potential for development.

- Assessing their parents' racing history and genetic lineage becomes crucial in determining their potential.

Prime Age:

- Pigeons between one to four years of age are considered to be in their prime racing years.
- At this age, they have the right balance of maturity and physical fitness.

Veterans:

- Older pigeons, while experienced, may have varying levels of physical fitness.
- Consider the individual racing history and overall health of veteran pigeons.

Balancing age considerations is vital when selecting racing pigeons. While young birds may have untapped potential, prime-aged pigeons strike the ideal balance of maturity and fitness, while veterans bring experience and may continue to perform well if in good health.

Conclusion: Crafting a Winning Team

In conclusion, selecting healthy and fit racing pigeons is an art that combines observation, examination, and a deep understanding of the intricate factors that contribute to success on the racecourse. From physical attributes and vital statistics to behavioral traits and age considerations, each element plays a crucial role in crafting a winning team of racing pigeons.

As enthusiasts embark on the journey of selecting pigeons for their loft, the goal is not just to assemble a team of athletes but to nurture a community of individuals whose health, genetic potential, and spirit align with the pursuit of victory.

A Comprehensive Guide to Feeding and Nutrition for Racing Pigeons

In the exhilarating world of pigeon racing, success on the racecourse is not just a result of training and genetics; it's also a reflection of optimal feeding and nutrition. This chapter delves into the essential aspects of crafting a nutrition plan that fuels the flight, supporting the health, endurance, and performance of racing pigeons.

1. Understanding the Pigeon Diet: The Foundation of Health

Seed Mixtures:

- A well-balanced seed mixture is the cornerstone of a racing pigeon's diet.
- Include a variety of seeds such as peas, maize, wheat, and barley to ensure a diverse nutrient intake.

Protein Sources:

- Pigeons require high-quality protein for muscle development and endurance.
- Incorporate sources like peas, lentils, and legumes to supplement the protein content in the diet.

Minerals and Grit:

- Essential minerals, particularly calcium and grit, aid in digestion and bone health.

- Provide access to grit and mineral supplements to meet these specific nutritional needs.

Understanding the basic components of a pigeon's diet is crucial for crafting a nutrition plan that meets their unique requirements. A balanced mixture of seeds, protein sources, and essential minerals forms the foundation for optimal health and performance.

2. The Racing Pigeon Nutrition Pyramid: Building Blocks of Performance

Base Layer: Seeds and Grains

- The majority of a pigeon's diet should consist of a high-quality seed mixture.
- Include a variety of seeds to provide a broad spectrum of essential nutrients.

Middle Layer: Protein Sources

- Introduce protein-rich sources like peas, lentils, and legumes.
- Protein is crucial for muscle development, energy production, and overall endurance.

Top Layer: Supplements and Specialized Feeds

- Enhance the diet with specialized feeds, supplements, and additives.
- Vitamin and mineral supplements, probiotics, and specific racing mixes can be incorporated based on individual needs.

The nutrition pyramid serves as a visual guide to understanding the proportional distribution of key nutritional components in a racing pigeon's diet. Balancing seeds, protein sources, and specialized feeds ensures a comprehensive and well-rounded nutrition plan.

3. The Role of Carbohydrates: Energy for Endurance

Complex Carbohydrates:

- Provide complex carbohydrates like barley and maize to supply sustained energy.
- These carbohydrates serve as a vital source of energy during long-distance flights.

Simple Carbohydrates:

- Include sources of simple carbohydrates for quick energy bursts.
- Raisins, figs, and honey can be added to the diet to provide readily available energy.

Carbohydrates play a crucial role in providing the energy required for endurance flights. The inclusion of both complex and simple carbohydrates in the diet ensures a balance between sustained energy and quick bursts of vitality.

4. Hydration: The Key to Performance

Clean and Fresh Water:

- Ensure pigeons have access to clean and fresh water at all times.
- Hydration is vital for digestion, metabolism, and overall performance.

Electrolyte Supplements:

- Introduce electrolyte supplements during periods of increased activity.
- Electrolytes aid in maintaining the balance of fluids and minerals, particularly during strenuous training and racing.

Proper hydration is fundamental to the health and performance of racing pigeons. Regular access to clean water and, when necessary, electrolyte supplements contribute to optimal hydration levels, ensuring pigeons are ready for the demands of training and racing.

5. Racing Season Nutrition: Adjusting for Peak Performance

Increasing Protein Intake:

- During the racing season, gradually increase the protein content in the diet.
- Elevated protein levels support muscle development and endurance during strenuous races.

Carbohydrate Loading:

- Implement carbohydrate loading strategies leading up to long-distance races.
- Providing an extra dose of complex carbohydrates helps pigeons build energy reserves for extended flights.

Post-Race Recovery:

- Include recovery feeds with added vitamins, minerals, and amino acids.
- These feeds aid in replenishing nutrients and supporting the recuperation of pigeons after demanding races.

Adapting the nutrition plan to the demands of the racing season is essential for maintaining peak performance. Adjusting protein intake, implementing carbohydrate loading, and prioritizing post-race recovery feeds contribute to the overall success of racing pigeons.

6. Individualized Nutrition Plans: Tailoring Diets for Excellence

Observation and Monitoring:

- Regularly observe pigeons for signs of health, energy levels, and performance.
- Individualized nutrition plans can be crafted based on specific needs and responses to dietary changes.

Consulting with Experts:

- Seek guidance from experienced pigeon fanciers and avian veterinarians.
- Professional insights can help refine nutrition plans to address individual variations in health and performance.

Recording and Adjusting:

- Maintain detailed records of dietary changes and performance outcomes.
- Use this information to continually refine and adjust individualized nutrition plans.

Recognizing that each racing pigeon is unique, tailoring nutrition plans based on individual needs is crucial for achieving excellence on the racecourse. Regular observation, expert consultation, and meticulous record-keeping contribute to the ongoing refinement of diets for optimal performance.

7. Common Nutritional Challenges: Identifying and Addressing Issues

Deficiency Symptoms:

- Be vigilant for signs of nutritional deficiencies, such as dull feathers, lethargy, or poor performance.
- Identify and address deficiencies promptly with targeted dietary adjustments or supplements.

Overfeeding and Obesity:

- Monitor pigeons for signs of overfeeding and obesity, which can impact performance.
- Adjust feeding amounts and introduce more exercise to maintain optimal body condition.

Digestive Issues:

- Introduce probiotics to support digestive health.
- Probiotics aid in maintaining a healthy gut flora and optimizing nutrient absorption.

Navigating common nutritional challenges is an integral part of maintaining the health and performance of racing pigeons. Identifying deficiency symptoms, managing body condition, and supporting digestive health contribute to a well-rounded nutrition strategy.

Conclusion: Sustaining Soaring Success

In conclusion, feeding and nutrition for racing pigeons is not a one-size-fits-all endeavor; it's an art that requires a deep understanding of the unique needs of each athlete. Crafting a nutrition plan that balances seeds, proteins, carbohydrates, and supplements is essential for supporting the health, endurance, and performance of racing pigeons.

As enthusiasts embark on the journey of pigeon racing, the role of nutrition becomes a vital component in the pursuit of success. So, with a keen eye on dietary intricacies and a commitment to tailoring nutrition plans for excellence, let the pigeons be fueled not just with food but with the precise blend of nutrients that propels them to soaring success on the wings of victory.

A Comprehensive Guide to Understanding Pigeon Health and Preventing Common Issues

In the dynamic world of pigeon racing, the pursuit of victory is intricately tied to the health and well-being of the feathered athletes. This chapter aims to unravel the nuances of pigeon health, offering insights into recognizing signs of well-being, common health issues, and proactive measures to prevent and address potential challenges. As we delve into this avian journey, the overarching goal is to empower pigeon fanciers with the knowledge needed to ensure their racing pigeons soar in the pink of health.

1. The Art of Observation: Decoding Signs of Well-Being

Plumage and Appearance:

- Shiny and well-groomed feathers are indicative of good health.
- Dull or ruffled feathers may signal underlying health issues, stress, or malnutrition.

Activity Levels:

- Energetic and lively behavior suggests a healthy pigeon.

- Lethargy, a lack of activity, or sitting puffed up for extended periods may be signs of illness.

Eyes and Nares:

- Clear and bright eyes are a positive indicator of health.
- Watery or swollen eyes, as well as any nasal discharge, may be signs of respiratory issues.

Observing pigeons keenly on a daily basis forms the foundation for understanding their baseline health. Recognizing subtle changes in plumage, behavior, and physical appearance enables pigeon fanciers to identify potential health concerns at an early stage.

2. Respiratory Health: Navigating Common Issues

Recognizing Respiratory Issues:

- Wheezing, coughing, or labored breathing are signs of respiratory distress.
- Pigeons with respiratory issues may display a reluctance to fly or reduced endurance.

Prevention Strategies:

- Provide well-ventilated lofts to minimize the risk of respiratory infections.
- Regular cleaning and disinfection of lofts contribute to a healthy respiratory environment.

Common Respiratory Conditions:

- Ornithosis and respiratory adenoviruses are prevalent respiratory infections.
- Timely veterinary intervention and quarantine measures can prevent the spread of these conditions.

Maintaining optimal respiratory health is crucial for racing pigeons, as their performance is directly impacted by the efficiency of their respiratory system. Recognizing signs of respiratory distress and implementing preventive measures are essential in mitigating common respiratory issues.

3. Gastrointestinal Health: Balancing Digestive Harmony

Signs of Digestive Issues:

- Changes in droppings, such as discoloration or consistency, may indicate digestive problems.
- Loss of appetite, weight loss, or abdominal swelling are potential signs of gastrointestinal issues.

Preventive Measures:

- Ensure access to clean and fresh water at all times.
- Provide a balanced and easily digestible diet to support healthy digestion.

Common Gastrointestinal Conditions:

- Coccidiosis and canker are prevalent gastrointestinal infections.
- Regular fecal examinations, proper loft hygiene, and targeted treatments can prevent and address these conditions.

A harmonious digestive system is crucial for the overall health of racing pigeons. Regular monitoring of droppings, maintaining proper hydration, and a balanced diet contribute to gastrointestinal well-being and prevent common issues.

4. Parasite Management: Safeguarding Against Infestations

External Parasites:

- Mites and lice can cause discomfort and stress to pigeons.
- Regular inspections and appropriate treatments help prevent external parasite infestations.

Internal Parasites:

- Worms, particularly roundworms and tapeworms, can affect digestive health.
- Scheduled deworming and proper loft hygiene are key preventive measures.

Resistant Strains:

- Resistance to certain parasite treatments can develop over time.
- Rotate and use a variety of effective parasite control methods to prevent the emergence of resistant strains.

Parasite management is a critical aspect of pigeon health. Regular inspections, targeted treatments, and a proactive approach to preventing both external and internal parasites contribute to the overall well-being of racing pigeons.

5. Immunization Protocols: Fortifying Pigeon Health

Vaccination Schedule:

- Follow a well-defined vaccination schedule recommended by avian veterinarians.
- Vaccinations protect against common diseases and contribute to overall immune system health.

Preventive Measures:

- Implement biosecurity measures to reduce the risk of disease introduction.
- Quarantine new pigeons before introducing them to the loft to prevent the spread of potential infections.

Common Pigeon Vaccines:

- Vaccines for paramyxovirus, pigeon pox, and salmonella are commonly administered.
- Avian veterinarians can tailor vaccination plans based on regional disease prevalence and loft-specific conditions.

Immunization plays a pivotal role in fortifying pigeon health and preventing the spread of contagious diseases. Following a well-structured vaccination schedule and implementing preventive measures contribute to the creation of a resilient and disease-resistant flock.

6. Stress Management: Nurturing Mental and Physical Well-Being

Recognizing Stressors:

- Changes in loft dynamics, environmental factors, or racing schedules can induce stress.

- Pigeons may exhibit stress through altered behavior, reduced appetite, or increased susceptibility to illness.

Minimizing Stress Factors:

- Maintain a consistent loft environment and routine to reduce stress.
- Gradual acclimatization to new conditions and minimizing disruptions contribute to stress reduction.

Providing Enrichment:

- Offer mentally stimulating activities, such as puzzle feeders or aviary access.
- Mental stimulation promotes well-being and alleviates stress.

Stress management is essential for maintaining the overall health and performance of racing pigeons. Identifying stressors, minimizing their impact, and providing enrichment activities contribute to a harmonious and stress-free loft environment.

7. Veterinary Partnership: Collaborating for Pigeon Well-Being

Regular Health Checkups:

- Schedule regular health checkups with an avian veterinarian.
- Routine examinations help detect and address potential health issues at an early stage.

Diagnostic Testing:

- Utilize diagnostic tests, such as blood tests and fecal examinations, to assess health parameters.

- Diagnostic testing aids in early detection and targeted treatment planning.

Emergency Preparedness:

- Establish an emergency plan in collaboration with the avian veterinarian.
- Timely access to veterinary care during emergencies is crucial for pigeon well-being.

Collaborating with an avian veterinarian is a cornerstone of comprehensive pigeon health management. Regular health checkups, diagnostic testing, and emergency preparedness form a holistic approach to ensuring the well-being of racing pigeons.

Conclusion: Nurturing the Wings of Victory

In conclusion, understanding pigeon health and preventing common issues is a multifaceted journey that combines observation, preventive measures, and collaboration with avian veterinarians. By unraveling the intricacies of respiratory, gastrointestinal, and overall health, pigeon fanciers can embark on a path that nurtures the wings of victory.

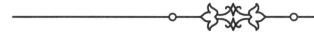

Chapter 3: Training Techniques for Racing Pigeons

Crafting Peak Fitness for Racing Pigeons

In the heart-pounding realm of pigeon racing, where every flap of a feather counts, the conditioning and fitness of racing pigeons are paramount. This chapter unfolds the art and science of sculpting winged athletes, exploring the nuances of training routines, exercise regimes, and nutritional strategies that propel these avian competitors to the pinnacle of performance. As we delve into the world of conditioning and fitness for racing pigeons, the overarching aim is to equip enthusiasts with the knowledge to elevate their feathered champions to soaring success.

1. The Foundations of Pigeon Fitness: A Holistic Approach

Understanding Pigeon Physiology:

- Pigeons are endurance athletes, with a natural ability for sustained flight.
- Their cardiovascular and respiratory systems are finely tuned for long-distance flights.

Balancing Mental and Physical Fitness:

- Mental well-being is integral to physical performance.
- A comfortable loft environment, positive interactions, and mental stimulation contribute to overall fitness.

Assessing Individual Fitness Levels:

- Regularly evaluate pigeons for signs of health and fitness.
- Tailor training programs based on individual fitness levels and responses.

Before delving into specific fitness routines, it's essential to recognize the holistic nature of pigeon fitness. Understanding their physiology, balancing mental and physical health, and assessing individual fitness levels form the foundational principles of crafting a successful fitness program.

2. Building Endurance: The Backbone of Pigeon Racing

Gradual Distance Increases:

- Gradually increase flying distances during training sessions.
- Building endurance is a progressive process that minimizes the risk of overexertion.

Variable Training Routes:

- Introduce variability in training routes and terrains.
- Exposure to diverse flight conditions enhances adaptability and endurance.

Long-Distance Training Flights:

- Schedule periodic long-distance training flights.
- These flights simulate race conditions, preparing pigeons for the physical and mental demands of competitions.

Endurance is the cornerstone of pigeon racing success. Training routines that focus on gradual distance increases, varied routes, and long-distance flights contribute to the development of resilient and enduring racing pigeons.

3. Interval Training: Enhancing Speed and Stamina

Sprint Intervals:

- Incorporate short, high-intensity flight intervals during training.
- Sprint intervals enhance speed and improve the cardiovascular fitness of racing pigeons.

Rest and Recovery:

- Allow sufficient rest between interval training sessions.
- Adequate recovery time is crucial for pigeons to build stamina and prevent overtraining.

Progressive Intensity:

- Gradually increase the intensity and duration of interval training.
- Progressive intervals challenge pigeons to improve their speed and stamina over time.

Interval training is a strategic component of pigeon fitness routines, targeting both speed and stamina. The incorporation of short bursts of high-intensity flight followed by adequate rest periods helps pigeons build the necessary cardiovascular and muscular adaptations for racing success.

4. Loft Exercise and Aviary Time: Maintaining Muscle Tone

Loft Flying:

- Encourage regular loft flying to maintain muscle tone.

- Short flights within the loft space help pigeons stay active and engaged.

Aviary Access:

- Provide access to an aviary for additional exercise.
- Aviary time allows pigeons to stretch their wings, preen, and engage in natural behaviors.

Flight Challenges:

- Create flight challenges within the loft or aviary.
- Placing obstacles or introducing target points encourages pigeons to engage in purposeful flight.

In addition to formal training flights, maintaining muscle tone through loft exercise and aviary time is crucial for overall pigeon fitness. These activities not only contribute to physical health but also provide mental stimulation and prevent boredom.

5. Nutritional Support for Fitness: The Fuel for Flight

Balanced Diets:

- Provide a nutritionally balanced diet to support energy needs.
- A well-rounded diet ensures that pigeons have the necessary nutrients for optimal performance.

Supplements for Endurance:

- Consider supplements that support endurance and muscle recovery.

- Omega-3 fatty acids, amino acids, and vitamin B-complex supplements can aid in conditioning.

Hydration:

- Ensure access to clean and fresh water at all times.
- Proper hydration is vital for energy metabolism and overall performance.

Nutritional support is an integral part of pigeon fitness routines. A balanced diet, strategic supplements, and proper hydration contribute to the overall conditioning and endurance of racing pigeons, ensuring they have the fuel they need for successful flights.

6. Monitoring and Adjusting Training Programs: The Art of Fine-Tuning

Performance Evaluation:

- Regularly assess the performance of pigeons during training flights.
- Record flight times, speed, and any signs of fatigue or distress.

Adjusting Training Intensity:

- Tailor training programs based on individual responses.
- Adjust flying distances, intervals, and rest periods to optimize fitness levels.

Seasonal Adjustments:

- Modify training programs based on the racing season.

- Gradually increase training intensity and distances leading up to important races.

Fine-tuning training programs requires a keen eye for performance evaluation and a willingness to adjust based on individual responses. Monitoring pigeons during training flights and making seasonal adjustments contribute to the ongoing refinement of fitness routines.

7. Mental Well-Being: The X-Factor in Racing Success

Positive Loft Environment:

- Foster a positive loft environment to support mental well-being.
- Minimize stressors and provide a comfortable, secure space for pigeons.

Training as Mental Stimulation:

- View training sessions as mental stimulation.
- Engage pigeons in purposeful flights, challenges, and varied routines to keep them mentally active.

Individualized Attention:

- Recognize and address individual preferences and needs.
- Some pigeons may thrive on social interaction, while others prefer solitude.

Mental well-being is often the X-factor that sets apart champions in pigeon racing. Creating a positive loft environment, viewing training as mental stimulation, and providing individualized attention contribute to the mental resilience and focus needed for success.

Conclusion: Wings of Triumph

In conclusion, the journey of conditioning and fitness for racing pigeons is an intricate dance between science and intuition. By understanding the physiological nuances of pigeons, implementing diverse training routines, ensuring proper nutrition, and nurturing mental well-being, enthusiasts can craft a path for their feathered athletes to triumph in the exhilarating world of pigeon racing.

Nurturing and Building Strong Homing Instincts in Racing Pigeons

In the captivating world of pigeon racing, the homing instinct is the compass that guides these feathered athletes back to their lofts from distant race locations. This chapter explores the intricate art of nurturing and building strong homing instincts in racing pigeons, delving into the factors that influence this innate ability and providing insights into training techniques, loft management, and genetic considerations that contribute to the development of a robust homing instinct. As we embark on this journey of guiding wings, the goal is to empower pigeon fanciers with the knowledge to cultivate homing prowess in their avian companions.

1. Unveiling the Homing Instinct: Nature's Navigation System

Innate Navigation Skills:

- Pigeons possess an innate ability to navigate and find their way home.
- This homing instinct is a result of a combination of genetic factors and environmental cues.

Scientific Insights:

- Studies have revealed that pigeons utilize various sensory cues, including the Earth's magnetic field, sun position, and visual landmarks, to navigate.
- The hippocampus, a region of the brain associated with spatial memory, plays a crucial role in homing instincts.

Genetic Basis:

- The homing instinct is hereditary, passed down through generations.
- Pigeons with strong homing genetics are more likely to exhibit superior navigational abilities.

Understanding the homing instinct begins with recognizing it as a natural navigation system ingrained in the very essence of pigeons. Genetic factors, environmental cues, and the intricate workings of the avian brain collectively contribute to this remarkable ability.

2. Selective Breeding: Cultivating Homing Prowess in Bloodlines

Champion Bloodlines:

- Selective breeding focuses on perpetuating strong homing genetics.
- Pigeons with a history of consistent and accurate returns are favored for breeding.

Pedigree Analysis:

- Studying the pedigree of potential breeding pairs helps identify and amplify strong homing traits.
- Consistency in homing performance within a bloodline is a positive indicator.

Genetic Diversity:

- While emphasizing champion bloodlines, balance is crucial to maintain genetic diversity.
- A diverse gene pool enhances adaptability and resilience in racing pigeons.

Selective breeding is a cornerstone in cultivating and strengthening homing instincts. By strategically pairing pigeons with a history of precise returns, fanciers can perpetuate strong homing genetics, ultimately enhancing the navigational prowess of future generations.

3. Early Life Exposure: The Foundation of Homing Recognition

Loft Familiarity:

- Young pigeons should be exposed to their loft environment from an early age.
- Familiarity with loft surroundings creates a sense of home that forms the foundation of homing recognition.

Loft Orientation Flights:

- Allow young pigeons to embark on short orientation flights around the loft.
- These initial flights help pigeons establish visual and spatial connections with their home.

Gradual Distance Increases:

- Progressive training involves gradually increasing the distance of training flights.

- Young pigeons learn to associate their home loft with safety and comfort through this gradual exposure.

Early life exposure to the loft and gradual distance increases in training flights play a pivotal role in shaping the homing recognition of racing pigeons. These formative experiences contribute to the development of a strong and accurate homing instinct.

4. Familiarization with Race Routes: Mapping the Mental GPS

Visual Landmarks:

- Introduce pigeons to visual landmarks along race routes during training.
- Associating landmarks with specific flight paths enhances pigeons' mental mapping of race routes.

Orientation Training:

- Conduct orientation training flights along race routes to reinforce mental mapping.
- Pigeons learn to recognize and navigate key points along the racecourse.

Repetition and Reinforcement:

- Repeat orientation flights to reinforce the mental GPS of racing pigeons.
- Consistent exposure to race routes enhances the accuracy of homing instincts.

Familiarization with race routes is a critical aspect of building strong homing instincts. Through exposure to visual landmarks and orientation training, racing pigeons develop a mental GPS that guides them with precision back to their lofts from distant race locations.

5. Gradual Release and Return: Confidence in Independence

Gradual Release:

- Gradually release pigeons at increasing distances from the loft during training.
- This gradual progression builds confidence and reinforces the homing instinct.

Short-Distance Returns:

- Initially focus on short-distance training flights with prompt and successful returns.
- Positive reinforcement establishes confidence and strengthens the homing connection.

Progressive Challenges:

- Gradually increase the difficulty of training flights with longer distances and varied conditions.
- Progressive challenges enhance the adaptability and resilience of homing instincts.

Building strong homing instincts involves a phased approach, starting with gradual releases and short-distance returns. As pigeons gain confidence in their ability to navigate back to the loft, progressive challenges contribute to the development of robust and reliable homing instincts.

6. Loft Management for Homing Success: Creating a Safe Haven

Comfortable Loft Environment:

- Maintain a clean, comfortable, and secure loft environment.
- A well-kept loft provides a safe haven that reinforces the homing instinct.

Consistent Loft Routine:

- Establish a consistent loft routine for feeding, watering, and loft access.
- Predictable routines contribute to the mental mapping of home for racing pigeons.

Individual Loft Spaces:

- Provide individual loft spaces for each pigeon.
- Personalized spaces enhance the sense of ownership and attachment to the loft.

Loft management plays a crucial role in creating a safe and familiar haven for racing pigeons. A well-maintained loft, consistent routines, and individualized spaces contribute to the reinforcement of the homing connection.

7. Racing Experience: The Culmination of Homing Training

Gradual Entry into Races:

- Introduce pigeons to races gradually, starting with shorter distances.
- Progressive exposure to racing conditions refines and strengthens homing instincts.

Race Returns as Positive Reinforcement:

- Positive experiences with successful race returns reinforce the homing connection.
- Pigeons build confidence and a sense of accomplishment through each successful race.

Post-Race Recovery:

- Implement a structured post-race recovery routine.
- Careful recovery after races supports overall well-being and maintains the positive association with homing returns.

The culmination of homing training is the racing experience. Gradual entry into races, positive reinforcement through successful returns, and thoughtful post-race recovery contribute to the refinement and perfection of homing instincts in racing pigeons.

Conclusion: Wings Guided by Instinct

In conclusion, the art of nurturing and building strong homing instincts in racing pigeons is a harmonious blend of genetics, early life exposure, familiarization with race routes, loft management, and the culmination of racing experiences. As enthusiasts embark on this journey of guiding wings, may each flutter resonate with the ancient and instinctual navigation system that propels these avian athletes to triumphant returns.

A Comprehensive Guide to Flight Training for Racing Pigeons

In the exhilarating world of pigeon racing, where every beat of the wing counts, flight training stands as the cornerstone of success. This chapter unravels the art and science of flight training, spanning from fundamental exercises to advanced drills that elevate racing pigeons to the pinnacle of performance. As we delve into the skies of avian athleticism, the goal is to equip pigeon fanciers with the knowledge to sculpt wings into instruments of mastery, ensuring their feathered athletes navigate the racecourse with precision and grace.

1. The Essence of Flight Training: Unleashing Avian Potential

Unlocking Natural Instincts:

- Flight is an innate ability for pigeons.
- Flight training aims to tap into and enhance the natural instincts that drive pigeons to soar through the skies.

Building Physical Fitness:

- Flight is a comprehensive exercise that engages muscles, cardiovascular system, and respiratory functions.
- Regular flight training contributes to the overall physical fitness of racing pigeons.

Strengthening Mental Acuity:

- Flight training fosters mental sharpness and navigational skills.
- Pigeons develop spatial awareness, orientation, and adaptability through varied flight exercises.

Flight training is not merely an exercise regimen; it's a holistic approach that taps into the intrinsic potential of pigeons, building physical prowess and mental acuity that are crucial for success on the racecourse.

2. Basic Flight Exercises: Foundations of Avian Fitness

Loft Flights:

- Begin with short loft flights to build familiarity with the loft environment.
- Pigeons develop confidence in their flying abilities within the safe confines of the loft.

Circling Exercises:

- Encourage circling flights within the loft space.
- Circling exercises enhance maneuverability and strengthen wing muscles.

Short-Distance Training Flights:

- Gradually progress to short-distance training flights.
- These exercises introduce pigeons to the concept of navigation and returning to the loft from varying distances.

Basic flight exercises form the foundation of avian fitness, introducing pigeons to the essential skills of flying within the loft, circling maneuvers, and the initial stages of navigation.

3. Progressive Distance Training: Navigating the Expanding Horizon

Gradual Distance Increases:

- Incrementally increase the distance of training flights.
- Pigeons adapt to longer flights, refining their navigational abilities with each progressive step.

Orientation Flights:

- Conduct orientation flights along race routes to familiarize pigeons with key landmarks.
- Orienting pigeons to race routes enhances their ability to navigate during competitions.

Variable Training Routes:

- Introduce variability in training routes and terrains.
- Pigeons learn to adapt to diverse flying conditions, further refining their navigational skills.

Progressive distance training is a pivotal phase in flight training, expanding the horizons for racing pigeons. Gradual increases in distance, orientation flights, and exposure to varied routes contribute to the development of seasoned aviators.

4. Speed Training: Enhancing Racing Performance

Sprint Exercises:

- Incorporate sprint exercises during training flights.
- Short bursts of high-intensity flight enhance speed and agility.

Timing and Racing Drills:

- Implement timing exercises to simulate race conditions.
- Pigeons learn to pace themselves and optimize their flight speed.

Competition Simulations:

- Organize mock races or friendly competitions among loft mates.
- Simulating racing scenarios sharpens pigeons' competitive edge and race-day readiness.

Speed training drills are designed to enhance the racing performance of pigeons, incorporating elements of sprint exercises, timing drills, and simulated race conditions to elevate their speed and competitiveness.

5. Altitude Training: Elevating Flight Endurance

Gradual Altitude Increases:

- Introduce gradual increases in flight altitude during training.
- Altitude training enhances respiratory and cardiovascular endurance.

High-Altitude Flights:

- Implement flights at higher altitudes to challenge endurance levels.
- Pigeons develop the stamina needed for long-distance races through high-altitude training.

Balancing Altitude and Speed:

- Strike a balance between altitude and speed training.
- Pigeons learn to optimize their flight strategy based on varying altitudes.

Altitude training is a strategic component aimed at elevating the endurance levels of racing pigeons. Gradual increases, high-altitude flights, and a balanced approach contribute to enhanced flight stamina.

6. Advanced Maneuver Drills: Precision in Flight

Aerial Obstacle Courses:

- Create aerial obstacle courses within the loft or aviary.

- Pigeons engage in precision flight maneuvers, enhancing agility and control.

Formation Flying:

- Introduce formation flying exercises with loft mates.
- Precision flying in formation enhances coordination and adaptability.

In-Flight Challenges:

- Incorporate challenges such as rapid direction changes or controlled landings.
- Advanced maneuver drills refine pigeons' flight control and responsiveness.

Advanced maneuver drills are designed to take flight training to a higher level, focusing on precision, agility, and control. Aerial obstacle courses, formation flying, and in-flight challenges contribute to the mastery of flight.

7. Weather Adaptation: Preparing for Variable Conditions

Flight in Adverse Weather:

- Gradually expose pigeons to flights in varying weather conditions.
- Training in adverse weather enhances adaptability and resilience.

Wind Resistance Training:

- Incorporate flights against the wind to build resistance.

- Pigeons learn to navigate and maintain speed in challenging wind conditions.

Rain and Storm Simulations:

- Simulate rain and storm conditions during training.
- Weather simulations prepare pigeons for unexpected challenges during races.

Weather adaptation drills prepare racing pigeons for the unpredictable conditions they may encounter during races. Exposure to adverse weather, wind resistance training, and rain simulations contribute to the development of resilient and adaptable aviators.

Conclusion: Soaring to Victory

In conclusion, flight training for racing pigeons is a dynamic journey that progresses from basic exercises to advanced maneuvers, encompassing elements of physical fitness, mental acuity, and strategic preparation for race conditions. As enthusiasts guide their feathered companions through loft flights, distance training, speed drills, altitude challenges, advanced maneuvers, and weather adaptations, may each beat of the wing resonate with the pursuit of mastery.

A Guide to Introducing Racing Pigeons to Different Weather Conditions

In the dynamic realm of pigeon racing, where the unpredictability of weather is a constant companion, the ability of racing pigeons to navigate diverse weather conditions is a crucial aspect of their success. This chapter explores the intricacies of introducing racing pigeons to different weather conditions, offering insights into the impact of weather on racing performance, training strategies for diverse weather scenarios, and the importance of acclimatization. As we embark on this meteorological journey, the goal is to equip pigeon fanciers with the knowledge to ensure their feathered athletes soar with confidence and resilience, regardless of the weather they encounter.

1. Weather as a Racing Variable: Understanding the Impact

Temperature and Performance:

- Temperature variations can impact the performance of racing pigeons.
- Pigeons tend to perform best in moderate temperatures, while extreme heat or cold can affect endurance.

Wind and Navigation:

- Wind direction and speed play a significant role in navigation.
- Tailwinds can enhance speed, while headwinds pose challenges and require additional effort.

Rain and Flight Conditions:

- Rain can affect flight conditions and visibility.
- Pigeons may alter their flight patterns in response to rain, affecting racing strategies.

Understanding the impact of weather variables is the first step in preparing racing pigeons for diverse conditions. Temperature, wind, and rain can influence performance, navigation, and flight patterns, necessitating a nuanced approach to training and acclimatization.

2. Monitoring Weather Forecasts: A Strategic Approach

Utilizing Weather Apps and Websites:

- Stay informed about weather forecasts through dedicated apps and websites.
- Regular updates on temperature, wind direction, and precipitation aid in planning training sessions.

Long-Range Forecast Planning:

- Plan training schedules based on long-range weather forecasts.
- Anticipate changes in weather conditions and adjust training routines accordingly.

Adaptability in Training Plans:

- Be flexible in adapting training plans based on real-time weather updates.
- Adjust flight distances, intensity, and routes to align with current weather conditions.

Monitoring weather forecasts is a strategic approach to weather adaptation. Utilizing technology, planning based on long-range forecasts, and maintaining adaptability in training plans enable fanciers to stay ahead of weather variations.

3. Temperature Acclimatization: Balancing the Thermometer

Gradual Exposure to Temperature Changes:

- Gradually expose pigeons to temperature changes during training.
- This helps pigeons acclimatize to varying temperatures without undue stress.

Shelter Options in Extreme Conditions:

- Provide shelter options in extreme temperatures.
- Shade and shelter allow pigeons to regulate their exposure to heat or cold.

Hydration in Heat:

- Emphasize hydration during hot weather.
- Pigeons may require additional water intake to stay hydrated in warm conditions.

Temperature acclimatization is essential for racing pigeons to navigate varying climates. Gradual exposure, shelter options, and specific considerations for hydration in extreme temperatures contribute to their adaptability.

4. Wind Navigation: Tailwinds and Headwinds

Strategic Flight Planning:

- Plan training flights with consideration for wind direction.
- Tailwinds can enhance speed, while headwinds may require adjustments in flight strategy.

Training in Diverse Wind Conditions:

- Expose pigeons to diverse wind conditions during training.
- Familiarity with flying in different wind speeds and directions enhances adaptability.

Optimizing Tailwinds:

- Strategically utilize tailwinds during races.

- Planning flight routes that align with favorable tailwinds can improve racing performance.

Wind navigation is a skill that racing pigeons must master. Strategic flight planning, exposure to diverse wind conditions, and optimization of tailwinds contribute to the development of navigational prowess in different wind scenarios.

5. Rainy Day Strategies: Flight Adaptations and Loft Considerations

Flight Adaptations in Rain:

- Observe how pigeons adapt their flight patterns during rain.
- Pigeons may fly lower or alter their route to mitigate the impact of rain.

Wet Feather Prevention:

- Implement measures to prevent wet feather conditions.
- Wet feathers can affect flight efficiency; providing shelter and loft conditions that prevent soaking helps maintain optimal flight conditions.

Post-Rain Recovery:

- Implement a structured post-rain recovery routine.
- Ensuring that pigeons recover effectively after flying in rain supports overall well-being.

Rainy days present unique challenges that require both flight adaptations and loft considerations. Observing pigeons in rain, preventing wet feather conditions, and implementing post-rain recovery routines contribute to the overall resilience of racing pigeons.

6. Snow and Winter Preparations: Adapting to Cold Conditions

Gradual Exposure to Cold Temperatures:

- Gradually expose pigeons to colder temperatures during winter.
- Acclimatization to cold conditions is essential for winter racing.

Winter Loft Management:

- Ensure that lofts are well-insulated and provide warmth in winter.
- Protecting pigeons from extreme cold conditions is crucial for their well-being.

Adjusting Flight Intensity:

- Modify flight intensity during winter training.
- Pigeons may adjust their flying patterns in response to colder temperatures.

Winter brings its own set of challenges, requiring a specialized approach to acclimatization. Gradual exposure, winter loft management, and adjusting flight intensity are key elements in preparing racing pigeons for cold weather conditions.

7. Simulating Race Day Conditions: Mimicking the Challenge

Mock Races in Varied Conditions:

- Organize mock races that simulate diverse weather conditions.

- This provides pigeons with exposure to the challenges they may encounter on race days.

Strategic Weather Simulations:

- Introduce strategic weather simulations during training.
- Simulating race day conditions helps pigeons adapt to potential challenges.

Performance Analysis and Adjustment:

- Analyze performance in simulated race conditions.
- Adjust training plans based on insights gained from simulations.

Simulating race day conditions during training is a proactive approach to weather adaptation. Mock races, strategic weather simulations, and performance analysis contribute to fine-tuning training plans based on real-world challenges.

Conclusion: Resilient Wings in Every Weather

In conclusion, introducing racing pigeons to different weather conditions is a dynamic and strategic process that requires careful planning, adaptability, and a deep understanding of the impact of weather variables on avian performance. As fanciers guide their feathered companions through temperature changes, wind variations, rainy days, winter conditions, and simulated race day challenges, may each flight be a testament to the resilience of wings against the ever-changing canvas of the sky.

Chapter 4: Racing Strategies and Competing at the Highest Level

A Comprehensive Guide to Participating in Pigeon Racing Competitions

In the riveting world of pigeon racing, the thrill of competition, the rush of wings against the wind, and the pursuit of victory create a tapestry of excitement for enthusiasts. This chapter unfolds the intricacies of participating in pigeon racing competitions, offering insights into race preparation, race day strategies, loft management, and the journey from novice to seasoned competitor. As we navigate the skies of competition, the goal is to equip pigeon fanciers with the knowledge to make each race a soaring testament to the dedication, strategy, and partnership between fanciers and their feathered athletes.

1. The Racing Calendar: Charting the Course of Competitions

Understanding Racing Seasons:

- Pigeon racing typically follows a seasonal calendar.
- Racing seasons vary based on geographic locations, with spring and summer being common racing periods.

Local and National Races:

- Racing calendars include both local club races and national competitions.
- Local races offer a platform for novice participants, while national races showcase the best of the best.

Race Distance and Categories:

- Races vary in distance, from short sprints to long-distance challenges.

- Categories may include young bird races, old bird races, and special events.

Understanding the racing calendar is the first step in charting the course of competitions. Whether participating in local club races or aiming for national acclaim, enthusiasts must align their training and preparation with the specific characteristics of each racing season.

2. Preparing for Race Day: A Strategic Approach

Training Routines Leading Up to Races:

- Tailor training routines based on race distances and categories.
- Gradual increases in distance and intensity prepare pigeons for the specific demands of upcoming races.

Feeding and Nutrition:

- Adjust feeding strategies in the days leading up to races.
- Providing a well-balanced diet with an emphasis on energy-rich foods enhances race-day performance.

Health Assessments:

- Conduct pre-race health assessments.
- Ensure pigeons are in optimal health, addressing any issues that may impact their ability to race.

Preparation for race day is a strategic process that involves aligning training routines, optimizing nutrition, and conducting thorough health assessments. Each element contributes to the overall readiness of pigeons for the challenges they will face during competitions.

3. Loft Management: A Hub of Racing Readiness

Optimal Loft Conditions:

- Maintain clean and comfortable loft conditions.
- A well-kept loft serves as a hub for racing readiness, promoting both physical and mental well-being.

Individualized Loft Spaces:

- Provide individual loft spaces for each pigeon.
- Individual spaces enhance a sense of security and ownership, contributing to racing confidence.

Loft Familiarity:

- Ensure pigeons are familiar with their loft environment.
- Familiarity with loft spaces aids in rapid returns and reduces stress on race days.

Loft management is a critical aspect of racing readiness. Clean and comfortable lofts, individualized spaces, and loft familiarity contribute to a conducive environment that supports optimal performance during competitions.

4. Basketing and Shipping: Preparing for the Journey

Basketing Protocols:

- Adhere to basketing protocols set by race organizers.
- Basketing involves placing pigeons in race baskets, a crucial step in preparing them for transport to the release point.

Shipping to Race Release Point:

- Ensure pigeons are shipped safely and efficiently to the race release point.
- Timely and careful shipping minimizes stress on pigeons before the race.

Race Basket Familiarity:

- Familiarize pigeons with race baskets during training.
- Comfort with the basket environment contributes to a smoother transition on race day.

Basketing and shipping are integral components of race preparation. Following established protocols, ensuring safe shipping practices, and familiarizing pigeons with the race basket environment are key steps in preparing them for the journey ahead.

5. Race Day Strategies: Decoding the Flight Path

Weather Assessment:

- Assess weather conditions on race day.
- Weather factors such as wind direction, temperature, and precipitation influence flight strategies.

Release Point Considerations:

- Understand the location of the release point.
- Knowledge of the release point's terrain and landmarks aids in strategic flight planning.

Race Day Nutrition:

- Provide light and easily digestible food on race day.
- Pigeons should have access to water and nutrition that supports sustained flight.

Race day strategies involve decoding the flight path based on weather conditions, release point considerations, and optimal nutrition. Fanciers must be attuned to the specific challenges of each race day to maximize the performance of their racing pigeons.

6. Tracking and Timing: Precision in Racing Performance

Electronic Timing Systems:

- Utilize electronic timing systems for accurate race tracking.
- Electronic timing systems record the precise moment pigeons cross the finish line.

Record Keeping and Analysis:

- Maintain detailed records of race performances.
- Analyzing race data helps identify patterns, assess performance, and make informed adjustments.

Post-Race Recovery:

- Implement a structured post-race recovery routine.
- Careful recovery after races supports overall well-being and maintains positive associations with racing.

Tracking and timing are crucial elements in the precision of racing performance. Electronic systems, meticulous record-keeping, and thoughtful post-race recovery contribute to the ongoing refinement of racing strategies.

7. Learning from Races: The Journey to Mastery

Performance Analysis:

- Analyze race performances critically.
- Assess flight times, conditions, and any deviations from expected outcomes.

Adjusting Training Plans:

- Modify training plans based on race insights.
- Identify areas for improvement and tailor training routines accordingly.

Building Experience Over Time:

- Recognize that mastery in pigeon racing is a journey.
- Each race provides valuable experience that contributes to long-term success.

Learning from races is an ongoing process that involves critical performance analysis, strategic adjustments, and the acknowledgment that mastery in pigeon racing is built over time. Embracing the journey and continuously refining approaches contribute to a fancier's growth as a seasoned competitor.

Conclusion: Soaring to Victory in Every Race

In conclusion, participating in pigeon racing competitions is a dynamic and multifaceted journey that encompasses meticulous preparation, strategic planning, and a deep understanding of the nuances of racing. As fanciers guide their feathered companions through the racing calendar, prepare for race days, manage lofts, and decode the flight path on race days, may each competition be a soaring testament to the partnership between fanciers and their winged athletes.

Decoding Race Routes and Course Navigation in Pigeon Racing

In the enthralling world of pigeon racing, the art of navigation is paramount to success. This chapter delves into the intricacies of understanding race routes and course navigation, exploring the factors that influence pigeons' flight paths, the challenges presented by different terrains, and the role of natural and man-made landmarks in guiding these avian athletes to victory. As we embark on this aerial journey, the goal is to unravel the mysteries of the skies and equip pigeon fanciers with the knowledge to decipher race routes and enhance the navigational prowess of their racing pigeons.

1. Race Route Planning: The Blueprint of the Skies

Geographic Considerations:

- Race routes are carefully planned based on geographic features.

- Organizers select routes that challenge pigeons while ensuring a fair and safe competition.

Terrain Variations:

- Consideration of diverse terrains adds complexity to race routes.
- Pigeons must navigate through mountains, valleys, bodies of water, and urban landscapes.

Distance Gradations:

- Race routes vary in distance, from short sprints to long-distance challenges.
- Longer races may involve multiple checkpoints, adding an extra layer of complexity.

Race route planning involves a meticulous consideration of geographic features, terrain variations, and distance gradations. Understanding the blueprint of the skies is essential for both organizers and fanciers to appreciate the challenges that racing pigeons face on their journeys.

2. Terrain Challenges: Navigating Nature's Obstacles

Mountainous Regions:

- Mountainous terrains present both challenges and opportunities.
- Pigeons must navigate through valleys and over peaks, with wind patterns influenced by the landscape.

Water Crossings:

- Bodies of water, such as rivers or lakes, add a unique dimension to race routes.
- Pigeons may alter their flight patterns when crossing water, considering wind speed and direction.

Urban Landscapes:

- Navigating urban areas introduces man-made challenges.
- Pigeons must adapt to buildings, roads, and other structures that may impact flight paths.

Terrain challenges require pigeons to navigate through a diverse range of landscapes. From mountainous regions and water crossings to urban landscapes, each terrain presents unique obstacles that test the navigational skills of racing pigeons.

3. Wind Dynamics: The Silent Navigator in the Skies

Understanding Wind Patterns:

- Wind direction and speed play a crucial role in race route dynamics.
- Pigeons utilize tailwinds for speed but face challenges with headwinds that require additional effort.

Adapting to Wind Variability:

- Pigeons must adapt to changing wind patterns during races.
- Variable wind conditions may necessitate adjustments in flight strategy and pacing.

Tailwind Optimization:

- Strategic flight planning involves optimizing tailwinds for speed.
- Planning race routes that align with favorable tailwinds enhances racing performance.

Wind dynamics act as the silent navigator in the skies, influencing the speed, direction, and challenges faced by racing pigeons during competitions. Understanding wind patterns is essential for fanciers seeking to decode the intricacies of race routes.

4. Natural Landmarks: Nature's Guideposts in the Sky

Utilizing Mountains and Hills:

- Pigeons may use prominent mountains and hills as navigational landmarks.
- Recognizing these features aids in course navigation, especially in mountainous regions.

Rivers and Lakes as Reference Points:

- Bodies of water serve as natural reference points.
- Pigeons may follow river courses or use lakes as visual cues to maintain course direction.

Sun and Celestial Navigation:

- Pigeons may utilize the sun and celestial bodies for orientation.
- Understanding the position of the sun at different times of day aids pigeons in maintaining a sense of direction.

Natural landmarks play a pivotal role as guideposts in the sky. Mountains, rivers, lakes, and celestial bodies serve as visual cues that racing pigeons use to maintain course direction and navigate through diverse race routes.

5. Loft Familiarity: The Homing Instinct in Action

Utilizing Homing Instinct:

- Loft familiarity is a powerful tool in course navigation.
- Pigeons draw on their homing instinct, recognizing visual cues that lead them back to their lofts.

Release Point Recognition:

- Pigeons must recognize the release point at the beginning of a race.
- The release point serves as a crucial reference for pigeons to establish their initial course direction.

The Influence of Genetic Navigation:

- The homing instinct is influenced by genetic factors.
- Pigeons with strong homing genetics are more adept at recognizing and navigating race routes.

Loft familiarity and the homing instinct are integral components of course navigation. Pigeons draw on their innate ability to recognize their loft and release point, and the influence of genetic navigation further enhances their capacity to navigate race routes successfully.

6. Man-Made Landmarks: Urban Navigation Challenges

Adapting to Urban Structures:

- Urban landscapes present unique challenges for pigeons.
- Buildings, roads, and other structures may alter flight paths and require adaptive navigation.

Recognizing Distinctive Structures:

- Pigeons may recognize distinctive man-made landmarks.
- Towers, bridges, or other prominent structures can serve as visual cues in urban environments.

Light and Sound Navigation:

- Urban areas may impact traditional navigation cues.
- Pigeons may adapt by utilizing artificial lights or sounds as supplementary navigational aids.

Man-made landmarks pose challenges and opportunities for pigeons navigating through urban environments. Adapting to structures, recognizing distinctive landmarks, and even utilizing artificial lights or sounds are strategies employed by racing pigeons in urban navigation.

7. Technological Advances: GPS Tracking and Beyond

Integration of GPS Technology:

- Technological advancements have introduced GPS tracking in pigeon racing.
- GPS devices provide real-time tracking, allowing fanciers to monitor pigeons' positions during races.

Data Analysis for Optimization:

- Analyzing GPS data enables fanciers to optimize race strategies.
- Insights into flight paths, speeds, and deviations contribute to informed decision-making.

Exploring Future Technologies:

- Ongoing advancements may introduce new technologies for race route optimization.
- From drone assistance to advanced tracking systems, the future holds possibilities for further enhancing navigation.

Technological advances, particularly in GPS tracking, have revolutionized the way fanciers approach race route navigation. Real-time tracking and data analysis empower fanciers to make informed decisions and optimize strategies based on the performance of their racing pigeons.

Conclusion: A Symphony of Flight and Navigation Mastery

In conclusion, understanding race routes and course navigation in pigeon racing is akin to deciphering a symphony composed by the skies. The interplay of terrain challenges, wind dynamics, natural and man-made landmarks, loft familiarity, and technological advancements creates a rich tapestry of navigation mastery.

Fine-Tuning Your Pigeons for Peak Performance

In the captivating world of pigeon racing, achieving peak performance is the pursuit of every dedicated fancier. This chapter unveils the art and science of fine-tuning racing pigeons, exploring the multifaceted aspects of physical conditioning, nutrition, health management, and strategic training. As fanciers embark on the journey of sculpting their avian athletes into peak performers, the goal is to equip them with the knowledge to optimize every element that contributes to the soaring success of their racing pigeons.

1. Physical Conditioning: The Foundation of Peak Performance

Flight Exercise Regimen:

- A well-structured flight exercise regimen is fundamental to physical conditioning.
- Regular flights within the loft and progressive distance training build the necessary muscle strength and endurance for racing.

Loft Design for Physical Activity:

- Loft design plays a crucial role in encouraging physical activity.
- Ample loft space, perches, and loft furniture create an environment that stimulates natural behaviors and exercise.

Balancing Rest and Activity:

- Achieving peak performance requires a balance between rest and activity.

- Periods of rest allow pigeons to recover and rebuild, ensuring sustained performance over the racing season.

Physical conditioning forms the foundation of peak performance. Through a thoughtfully designed flight exercise regimen, loft environments that promote physical activity, and a balanced approach to rest, fanciers set the stage for the development of racing pigeons with optimal physical prowess.

2. Nutritional Excellence: Fueling the Flight to Victory

Balanced Diet Composition:

- A balanced diet is crucial for the overall health and performance of racing pigeons.
- Nutrient-rich grains, seeds, and supplements provide the necessary fuel for flight.

Pre-Race Nutrition:

- Tailoring nutrition before races is essential for peak performance.
- Pre-race meals should include energy-dense foods to sustain pigeons throughout the race.

Hydration Strategies:

- Hydration is a critical component of peak performance.
- Fanciers must ensure that pigeons have access to clean and fresh water at all times, with special attention to hydration before and after flights.

Nutritional excellence is the key to fueling the flight to victory. A balanced diet composition, pre-race nutrition strategies, and meticulous hydration plans contribute to the overall well-being and performance of racing pigeons.

3. Health Management: Vigilance for Racing Success

Regular Health Checks:

- Regular health checks are essential for identifying and addressing potential issues.
- Fanciers should monitor weight, plumage condition, and overall vitality to detect health concerns early.

Vaccination Protocols:

- Vaccination against common diseases is a preventive measure for peak performance.
- Fanciers must adhere to vaccination schedules to protect racing pigeons from potential health threats.

Quarantine Practices:

- Implementing quarantine practices for new arrivals is crucial.
- Isolating new pigeons before introducing them to the loft helps prevent the spread of diseases.

Vigilance in health management is a cornerstone of racing success. Regular health checks, vaccination protocols, and quarantine practices contribute to the overall well-being and resilience of racing pigeons, ensuring they are in prime condition for competitions.

4. Strategic Training: Sculpting Champions through Practice

Varied Training Routes:

- Varied training routes expose pigeons to diverse flying conditions.
- Fanciers should design training routes that mimic race scenarios, incorporating different terrains and challenges.

Mock Races and Simulations:

- Organizing mock races and simulations enhances race readiness.
- Pigeons benefit from exposure to simulated race conditions, allowing fanciers to assess and adjust strategies.

Speed and Endurance Drills:

- Incorporating speed and endurance drills fine-tunes racing abilities.
- Specific drills, such as sprint exercises and long-distance flights, contribute to the development of well-rounded athletes.

Strategic training is the sculptor's tool for crafting champions. Varied training routes, mock races, and speed/endurance drills shape racing pigeons into athletes equipped to handle the challenges of real competitions.

5. Mental Resilience: Sharpening the Competitive Edge

Positive Reinforcement:

- Positive reinforcement builds a strong mental connection between fancier and pigeon.
- Rewarding desired behaviors enhances the pigeons' motivation and confidence.

Environmental Enrichment:

- Environmental enrichment in the loft stimulates mental activity.
- Toys, perches, and loft structures that engage pigeons mentally contribute to overall resilience.

Handling and Loft Bonding:

- Gentle handling and regular loft bonding sessions strengthen the bond between fancier and pigeon.

- A strong bond fosters trust and a positive mindset, crucial for racing success.

Mental resilience is the secret weapon for a competitive edge. Positive reinforcement, environmental enrichment, and a strong bond between fancier and pigeon contribute to the mental fortitude needed for peak performance in the face of racing challenges.

6. Recovery and Rest: The Silent Architects of Victory

Structured Recovery Routines:

- Post-flight recovery routines are essential for peak performance.
- Structured recovery includes rest, hydration, and nutrition to support rapid recuperation.

Rest Periods Between Races:

- Adequate rest periods between races are crucial.
- Fanciers must strategically plan race schedules to allow pigeons sufficient time for recovery.

Seasonal Rest Cycles:

- Seasonal rest cycles contribute to long-term performance.
- Allowing pigeons extended periods of rest between racing seasons maintains overall health and longevity.

Recovery and rest are the silent architects of victory. Structured recovery routines, well-planned rest periods between races, and seasonal rest cycles contribute to the sustained peak performance and longevity of racing pigeons.

7. Data Analysis and Continuous Improvement: The Path to Mastery

Performance Data Tracking:

- Utilize data tracking systems to monitor race performances.
- Analyzing flight times, conditions, and deviations contributes to informed decision-making.

Adjustments to Training Plans:

- Modify training plans based on performance insights.
- Identifying areas for improvement allows fanciers to tailor training routines for optimal results.

Continuous Learning and Adaptation:

- Pigeon racing is a continuous learning journey.
- Fanciers must remain open to adapting strategies based on new insights and advancements in the field.

Data analysis and continuous improvement are the hallmarks of mastery. By tracking performance data, adjusting training plans, and embracing a mindset of continuous learning, fanciers pave the way for ongoing success and peak performance in pigeon racing.

Conclusion: Soaring to Victories Unimagined

In conclusion, fine-tuning racing pigeons for peak performance is an intricate dance between science, art, and unwavering dedication. As fanciers sculpt their avian athletes through physical conditioning, nutritional excellence, health management, strategic training, mental resilience, recovery, and continuous improvement, may each flight be a symphony of precision and triumph.

Crafting Strategies for Pigeon Racing Success

In the exhilarating world of pigeon racing, success is not merely a result; it's a carefully crafted journey that encompasses every facet of the fancier's expertise. This chapter delves into the intricate strategies that pave the way for success, from meticulous loft management and comprehensive training regimens to race day rituals that set the stage for triumph. As fanciers navigate the skies of competition, the goal is to illuminate the strategies that elevate racing pigeons from participants to champions, ensuring each flight is a step closer to victory.

1. Loft Management: The Command Center of Success

Cleanliness and Hygiene:

- A clean and hygienic loft is the foundation of success.
- Regular cleaning, disinfection, and pest control create an environment conducive to optimal health and performance.

Individualized Spaces:

- Providing individualized spaces for each pigeon fosters a sense of security.
- Individual perches and nesting areas reduce stress and contribute to a harmonious loft atmosphere.

Optimal Ventilation and Lighting:

- Ensuring optimal ventilation and natural lighting supports overall well-being.
- Well-ventilated lofts with adequate exposure to natural light contribute to the physical and mental health of racing pigeons.

Loft management serves as the command center from which success takes flight. A clean, organized, and well-maintained loft, coupled with individualized spaces and optimal ventilation, establishes the groundwork for racing pigeons to thrive.

2. Comprehensive Training Regimens: Sculpting Champions in the Skies

Progressive Flight Exercises:

- Designing progressive flight exercises builds essential muscle strength and endurance.
- Gradual increases in distance and intensity prepare racing pigeons for the demands of competitions.

Simulated Race Conditions:

- Incorporating simulated race conditions during training enhances race readiness.
- Mock races and diverse flying scenarios expose pigeons to the challenges they may encounter on actual race days.

Speed and Endurance Drills:

- Speed and endurance drills contribute to a well-rounded training regimen.
- Sprints, interval training, and long-distance flights fine-tune racing abilities for diverse race scenarios.

Comprehensive training regimens sculpt champions in the skies. Progressive flight exercises, simulated race conditions, and speed/endurance drills contribute to the development of racing pigeons ready to face the challenges of real competitions.

3. Strategic Nutrition: Fueling the Flight to Victory

Balanced Diet Composition:

- Crafting a balanced diet is crucial for peak performance.
- Nutrient-rich grains, seeds, and supplements provide the necessary fuel for flight.

Pre-Race Nutrition:

- Tailoring nutrition before races optimizes energy levels.

- Pre-race meals should include energy-dense foods to sustain pigeons throughout the race.

Hydration Strategies:

- Meticulous hydration plans contribute to overall well-being.
- Access to clean and fresh water is essential, with special attention to hydration before and after flights.

Strategic nutrition is the fuel that propels pigeons to victory. A balanced diet, tailored pre-race nutrition, and hydration strategies contribute to the overall well-being and performance of racing pigeons.

4. Health Vigilance: The Guardian of Racing Success

Regular Health Checks:

- Vigilant monitoring of weight, plumage, and overall vitality detects potential health issues early.
- Regular health checks are integral to preventing and addressing health concerns promptly.

Vaccination Protocols:

- Adhering to vaccination schedules safeguards against common diseases.
- Preventive measures contribute to the overall health and resilience of racing pigeons.

Quarantine Practices:

- Implementing quarantine practices for new arrivals prevents disease spread.
- Isolating new pigeons before introducing them to the loft is a crucial biosecurity measure.

Health vigilance is the guardian of racing success. Regular health checks, vaccination protocols, and quarantine practices contribute to the overall well-being and resilience of racing pigeons, ensuring they are in prime condition for competitions.

5. Mental Resilience: The X-Factor in Competitive Edge

Positive Reinforcement:

- Positive reinforcement builds a strong mental connection between fancier and pigeon.
- Rewarding desired behaviors enhances motivation and confidence.

Environmental Enrichment:

- Loft environments enriched with toys, perches, and structures stimulate mental activity.
- Mental engagement contributes to overall resilience and well-being.

Handling and Bonding:

- Gentle handling and regular bonding sessions strengthen the bond between fancier and pigeon.
- A strong bond fosters trust and a positive mindset, crucial for racing success.

Mental resilience is the X-factor in gaining a competitive edge. Positive reinforcement, environmental enrichment, and a strong bond between fancier and pigeon contribute to the mental fortitude needed for peak performance in the face of racing challenges.

6. Race Day Rituals: Preparing for Soaring Triumphs

Weather Assessment:

- Assessing weather conditions on race day is crucial.
- Wind direction, temperature, and precipitation influence race day strategies.

Release Point Familiarity:

- Ensuring pigeons are familiar with the release point is essential.
- Recognition of the release point aids in establishing the initial course direction.

Nutrition and Hydration:

- Providing light and easily digestible food on race day is key.
- Access to water and nutrition that supports sustained flight is a priority.

Race day rituals are the final preparations for soaring triumphs. Weather assessment, release point familiarity, and meticulous attention to nutrition and hydration set the stage for success as pigeons take to the skies in pursuit of victory.

7. Data Analysis and Continuous Improvement: The Mastery Path

Performance Data Tracking:

- Utilizing data tracking systems to monitor race performances is essential.
- Analyzing flight times, conditions, and deviations contributes to informed decision-making.

Adjustments to Training Plans:

- Modifying training plans based on performance insights is crucial.
- Identifying areas for improvement allows fanciers to tailor training routines for optimal results.

Continuous Learning and Adaptation:

- Embracing a mindset of continuous learning is key to success.
- Fanciers must remain open to adapting strategies based on new insights and advancements in the field.

Data analysis and continuous improvement pave the path to mastery. By tracking performance data, adjusting training plans, and embracing a mindset of continuous learning, fanciers ensure ongoing success and peak performance in pigeon racing.

Conclusion: Crafting the Symphony of Triumph

In conclusion, crafting strategies for pigeon racing success is an art that intertwines loft management, training regimens, nutrition, health vigilance, mental resilience, race day rituals, and continuous improvement. As fanciers master the symphony of these strategies, may each flight be a harmonious testament to the meticulous craftsmanship that defines the world of pigeon racing.

A Soaring Conclusion to the World of Pigeon Racing

In the vast and dynamic skies of pigeon racing, every loft, every fancier, and every feathered athlete contributes to a narrative that unfolds with each beat of wings. As we draw the curtains on this exploration into the captivating world of pigeon racing, it is fitting to reflect on the journey we've taken, the strategies we've uncovered, and the triumphs that echo in the lofted realms of victory.

1. A Tapestry of Dedication and Strategy

Pigeon racing is not just a sport; it is a tapestry woven with threads of dedication and strategy. Fanciers invest countless hours in the meticulous care of their feathered companions, shaping them into athletes ready to face the challenges of race day. The dedication of fanciers, combined with strategic approaches to loft management, training, nutrition, health, and mental resilience, creates a harmonious symphony that reverberates in every loft.

2. A Symphony of Precision in Training and Conditioning

The training regimens designed to sculpt champions are a testament to the precision and artistry involved in pigeon racing. From progressive flight exercises and simulated race conditions to speed and endurance drills, each training session is a brushstroke on the canvas of a racing pigeon's journey. The conditioning of these avian athletes is not just physical but also a mental preparation, fostering resilience and a competitive edge that elevates them to peak performance.

3. Fueling Success: The Science of Nutrition

Nutrition emerges as a cornerstone of success, fueling the flight to victory. Fanciers meticulously craft balanced diets, tailor nutrition for pre-race readiness, and ensure hydration strategies that sustain pigeons throughout their flights. The impact of strategic nutrition extends beyond mere sustenance; it is the fuel that propels pigeons to triumph and positions them as formidable contenders in the competitive arena.

4. The Guardian of Triumph: Vigilance in Health Management

Health vigilance stands as the guardian of triumph in pigeon racing. Regular health checks, adherence to vaccination protocols, and the implementation of quarantine practices safeguard against potential threats. Fanciers, acting as stewards of their pigeons' well-being, ensure that each athlete is in prime condition to face the rigors of competitions.

5. Mental Resilience: The Unseen Force in Victory

Mental resilience emerges as the unseen force that propels pigeons to victory. Positive reinforcement, environmental enrichment, and the bond forged between fancier and pigeon contribute to a mindset that transcends challenges. In the face of unpredictable race conditions, mental fortitude becomes the secret weapon that turns potential setbacks into opportunities for triumph.

6. Race Day Rituals: The Culmination of Preparation

Race day rituals mark the culmination of meticulous preparation. Weather assessments, release point familiarity, and attention to nutrition and hydration become the final acts before pigeons take flight. The rituals are not mere traditions but strategic maneuvers that set the stage for soaring triumphs, turning the loft into a theater where the drama of competition unfolds.

7. A Symphony of Data and Mastery

In the data-driven age, mastery in pigeon racing is not just an art; it is a science. Data analysis becomes the lens through which fanciers gain insights into flight times, conditions, and deviations. Continuous learning, adaptation, and adjustments to training plans are the threads that weave the fabric of mastery, ensuring that every race becomes an opportunity for refinement and improvement.

8. The Journey Continues: Unveiling New Horizons

As we conclude this exploration into the world of pigeon racing, it is essential to recognize that the journey continues. New horizons await fanciers and their feathered companions. Advancements in technology, evolving strategies, and a community of enthusiasts committed to the pursuit of excellence promise a future where the skies are limitless and victories are yet to be imagined.

Conclusion: Soaring Beyond the Horizon

In conclusion, pigeon racing is more than a sport; it is a celebration of dedication, strategy, and the indomitable spirit of both fanciers and pigeons. The loft becomes a stage where the drama of competition unfolds, and each flight is a chapter in the ongoing narrative of triumph. As fanciers and their athletes soar beyond the horizon, may the echoes of victory resound in every loft, reminding us that in the skies of pigeon racing, the journey is as exhilarating as the destination.

Books, Apps, and Websites for further research

Embarking on the fascinating journey of pigeon racing opens up a world of knowledge and resources that extend beyond the confines of a single book or guide. To further enrich your understanding and refine your skills as a pigeon fancier, explore a curated selection of books, apps, and websites that serve as valuable resources for in-depth research, insights, and community engagement.

Books:

1. **"Pigeon Racing: Handling, Health, Keeping, Housing, Breeding, Racing, and Training" by Elliott Lang:** This comprehensive guide covers various aspects of pigeon racing, from basic care to advanced training techniques. Lang's expertise provides a solid foundation for both beginners and experienced fanciers.
2. **"Pigeon Racing: Deep into Sport" by Dr. Wim Peters:** Dr. Peters, a renowned expert in pigeon racing, delves deep into the science and art of the sport. This book offers a blend of practical advice and scientific insights, making it a valuable addition to your racing pigeon library.
3. **"Secrets of the Racing Ace" by Wendell M. Levi:** This classic work explores the strategies and secrets employed by successful racing pigeon fanciers. Levi shares anecdotes, tips, and lessons learned from

seasoned veterans, providing a glimpse into the world of elite pigeon racing.

Apps:

1. **Pigeon Planner (iOS and Android):** Pigeon Planner is a versatile app that helps fanciers manage their loft and racing pigeon information. From tracking health records to monitoring training progress, this app is a handy tool for on-the-go management.
2. **Pigeon Racing Speed & Time Calculator (iOS and Android):** For the competitive enthusiast, this app assists in calculating racing speeds and times. It's a useful tool for analyzing race performance and strategizing for future competitions.
3. **Pigeon Loft Organizer (iOS):** This app is designed to streamline loft management, offering features for tracking breeding, health records, and racing results. Its user-friendly interface makes it a practical companion for fanciers seeking efficient organization.

Websites:

1. **American Racing Pigeon Union (ARPU) - pigeon.org:** The ARPU is a hub of information for pigeon racers, providing resources on loft management, race results, and industry news. It's a go-to platform for staying updated on the latest developments in the world of pigeon racing.
2. **Pigeon Paradise - pigeonparadise.com:** Pigeon Paradise is a comprehensive website offering articles, forums, and a marketplace for pigeon-related products.

Engage with a global community of fanciers, share experiences, and access a wealth of information on various aspects of pigeon racing.

3. **Pigeon Insider - pigeoninsider.com:** This website features articles, blogs, and forums where pigeon enthusiasts share tips, stories, and insights. It's a community-driven platform that fosters collaboration and knowledge exchange among fanciers.

Acknowledgment

Embarking on the journey of creating a guide on pigeon racing has been an enriching experience, and I extend my heartfelt gratitude to those who have played a pivotal role in bringing this project to fruition.

First and foremost, I want to express my sincere appreciation to the pigeon racing community—a vibrant and passionate group of enthusiasts whose dedication to the sport serves as an endless source of inspiration. Your shared knowledge, experiences, and camaraderie have been invaluable in shaping the content of this guide.

I extend my gratitude to the authors and experts whose works have served as guiding lights throughout the research process. Their contributions have provided depth and insight, enriching the content and ensuring its accuracy.

Special thanks go to the developers and creators of pigeon racing apps and websites, whose innovative tools have enhanced the accessibility and management of information in the world of pigeon racing. Your commitment to advancing the sport through technology is commendable.

I would also like to acknowledge the pigeon organizations and unions that tirelessly work to promote and regulate the sport. Your dedication to fostering a sense of community and ensuring fair competition is integral to the continued success of pigeon racing.

To friends, family, and colleagues who offered unwavering support and encouragement, thank you for being the pillars that sustained me throughout this endeavor. Your belief in the importance of sharing knowledge and fostering a love for pigeon racing has been a driving force.

Lastly, to the pigeons themselves—the true stars of this sport—thank you for being remarkable athletes and partners in this journey. Your instincts, resilience, and beauty have made the exploration of pigeon racing a truly captivating experience.

In closing, this acknowledgment is a reflection of the collaborative spirit that defines the world of pigeon racing. Each contribution, whether large or small, has played a vital role in creating a guide that I hope will inspire and inform fellow enthusiasts on their own pigeon racing adventures. Thank you to everyone who has been a part of this endeavor.

Freddie J.Craig

Freddie J.Craig

Before You Go

My final request...

Being a smaller author, reviews help me tremendously!

It would mean the world to me if you could leave a review.

If you liked reading this book and enjoyed some of it, please go to this link:

>> Please go and leave a brief review on Amazon.

It only takes 30 seconds, but it means so much to me! Thank you, and I can't wait to see your thoughts.

Printed in the USA
CPSIA information can be obtained
at www.ICGtesting.com
LVHW010012041124
795605LV00008B/519

9 798868 092145